D1627225

SNAKES ALIVE

Bull Snakes

by Ellen Frazel

BLASTOFF!
3
READERS

BELLWETHER MEDIA · MINNEAPOLIS, MN

Note to Librarians, Teachers, and Parents:

Blastoff! Readers are carefully developed by literacy experts and combine standards-based content with developmentally appropriate text.

Level 1 provides the most support through repetition of high-frequency words, light text, predictable sentence patterns, and strong visual support.

Level 2 offers early readers a bit more challenge through varied simple sentences, increased text load, and less repetition of high-frequency words.

Level 3 advances early-fluent readers toward fluency through increased text and concept load, less reliance on visuals, longer sentences, and more literary language.

Level 4 builds reading stamina by providing more text per page, increased use of punctuation, greater variation in sentence patterns, and increasingly challenging vocabulary.

Level 5 encourages children to move from "learning to read" to "reading to learn" by providing even more text, varied writing styles, and less familiar topics.

Whichever book is right for your reader, Blastoff! Readers are the perfect books to build confidence and encourage a love of reading that will last a lifetime!

This edition first published in 2012 by Bellwether Media, Inc.

No part of this publication may be reproduced in whole or in part without written permission of the publisher. For information regarding permission, write to Bellwether Media, Inc., Attention: Permissions Department, 5357 Penn Avenue South, Minneapolis, MN 55419.

Library of Congress Cataloging-in-Publication Data

Frazel, Ellen.
  Bull snakes / by Ellen Frazel.
    p. cm. – (Blastoff! Readers. Snakes alive)
  Includes bibliographical references and index.
  Summary: "Simple text and full-color photography introduce beginning readers to bull snakes. Developed by literacy experts for students in kindergarten through third grade"–Provided by publisher.
  ISBN 978-1-60014-613-8 (hardcover : alk. paper)
  1. Bullsnake–Juvenile literature. I. Title.
  QL666.O636F73 2011
  597.96'2–dc22
                            2011004208

Printed in the United States of America, North Mankato, MN.

080111   1187

Contents

Bull snakes are one of the largest snakes in the United States. They are named for the loud hiss they make. It sounds like a bull's **snort**.

Most bull snakes are between 4 and 8 feet (1.2 and 2.4 meters) long. They can weigh between 4 and 20 pounds (1.8 and 9.1 kilograms).

Bull snakes have **scales** on their bodies. They are yellowish with brown, black, or red patches. Black bands circle their tails.

Bull snakes look a lot like **poisonous** rattlesnakes. This helps keep **predators** away.

rattlesnake

= areas where bull snakes live

Bull snakes live in
many **habitats** in
the United States,
Mexico, and Canada.

They make homes in prairies, forests, and deserts. They dig **burrows** in sand and soil.

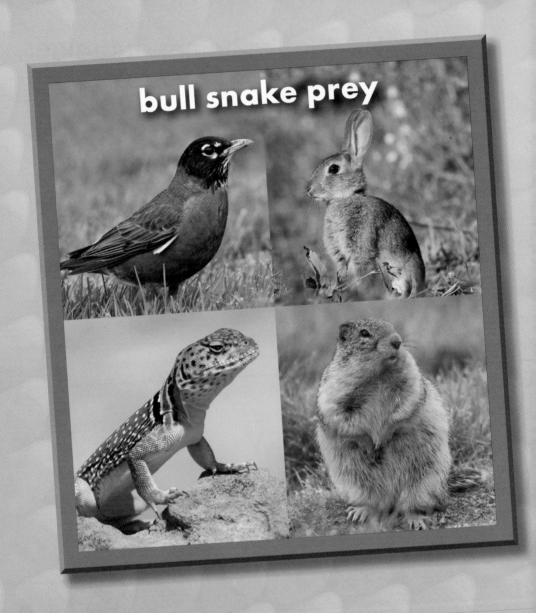

bull snake prey

Bull snakes hunt many types of **prey**. They eat birds, rabbits, lizards, and rodents.

Bull snakes have good **camouflage**. Their colors and patterns help them hide while they hunt.

Bull snakes stick out their forked
tongues to smell for prey. They attack
when an animal comes close.

Bull snakes also **slither** into burrows. They look for mice, gophers, and other small animals.

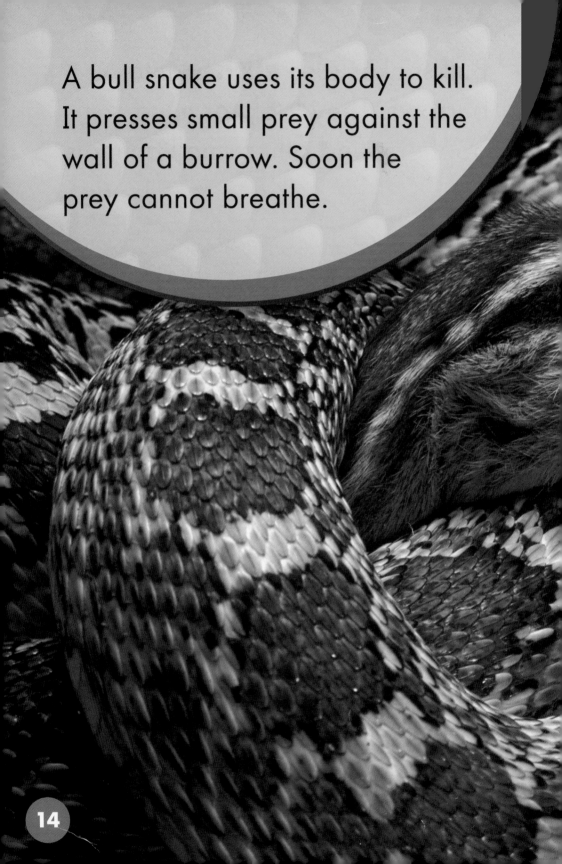

A bull snake uses its body to kill. It presses small prey against the wall of a burrow. Soon the prey cannot breathe.

A bull snake **coils** its body around large prey. It squeezes the prey until it stops moving. Then the bull snake swallows it whole!

Bull snakes can
be prey too.
They must watch
out for hawks,
foxes, and
other predators.

Bull snakes do not like to face predators. They hide when they **sense** a predator is near.

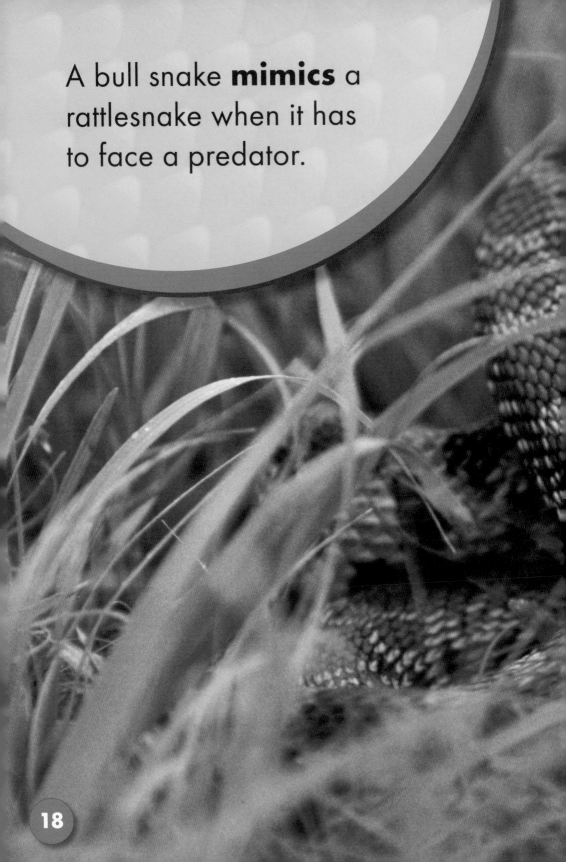

A bull snake **mimics** a rattlesnake when it has to face a predator.

It raises its body up into an S-shape. It hisses and hits its tail on the ground.

The bull snake
flattens its head and
throws it forward.
This looks like the
deadly **strike** of
a rattlesnake.

The predator runs away.
The bull snake has
tricked it!

Glossary

burrows—holes or tunnels in the ground made by animals

camouflage—coloring and patterns that hide an animal by making it look like its surroundings

coils—winds into loops; some snakes coil their bodies around their prey.

habitats—environments in which a plant or animal usually lives

mimics—acts like; a bull snake mimics a poisonous rattlesnake to scare predators.

poisonous—able to kill or harm with a poison

predators—animals that hunt other animals for food

prey—animals hunted by other animals for food

scales—small plates of skin that cover and protect a snake's body

sense—to become aware of

slither—to slide

snort—a loud noise made by pushing air through the nose; a bull snake's hiss sounds like the snort of a bull.

strike—to quickly throw the head and front part of the body at a predator or prey

To Learn More

AT THE LIBRARY
Butterfield, Moira. *Who Eats Who in Grasslands?*
North Mankato, Minn.: Smart Apple Media, 2007.

Rounds, Glen. *Mr. Yowder and the Giant Bull Snake.*
New York, N.Y.: Holiday House, 1978.

Tarbox, A. D. *A Prairie Food Chain.* Mankato, Minn.:
Creative Education, 2009.

ON THE WEB
Learning more about bull snakes
is as easy as 1, 2, 3.

1. Go to www.factsurfer.com.

2. Enter "bull snakes" into the search box.

3. Click the "Surf" button and you will see a list of
   related Web sites.

With factsurfer.com, finding more information is just a
click away.

Index

The images in this book are reproduced through the courtesy of: Jason Lugo/iStock, front cover, pp. 16-17; Sonya Greer/iStock, pp. 4 (small), 12; All Canada Photos/Alamy, pp. 4-5; Michelle Gilders/Alamy, pp. 6, 11, 20-21; Ron Kimball/KimballStock, p. 7; Jon Eppard, p. 8 (small); Tim Pleasant, pp. 8-9; Shutterstock, p. 10; Jim Merli/Getty Images, p. 13; James Gerholdt/Photolibrary, pp. 14-15; Juan Martinez, p. 16 (small); Phil Schermeister/Getty Images, pp. 18-19; Matt Behm, p. 20 (small).